My Scale Book

LATE ELEMENTARY–EARLY INTERMEDIATE

By **DAVID HIRSCHBERG**

My Scale Book offers piano students a series of graded scale exercises for the development of technic and musicianship. These scale studies will reinforce the technical requirements found in method books and in standard piano repertory. **My Scale Book** may be used with the **Technic Is Fun** series to assist students and performers in developing a strong musical and technical foundation.

Editor: Gail Lew

Production Coordinator: Sheryl Rose

Cover Design: Martha Lucia Ramirez

Contents

MAJOR SCALES - ONE OCTAVE

C Major

G Major

D Major

A Major

4

E Major

B Major

F Major

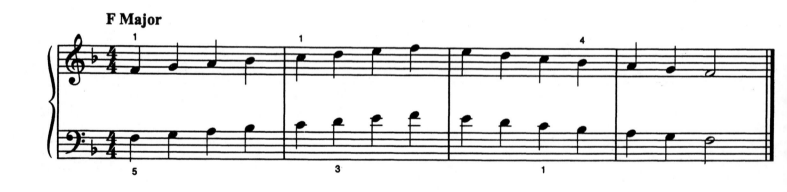

B♭ Major

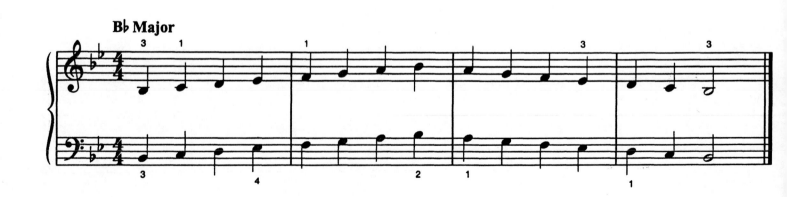

E♭ Major

A♭ Major

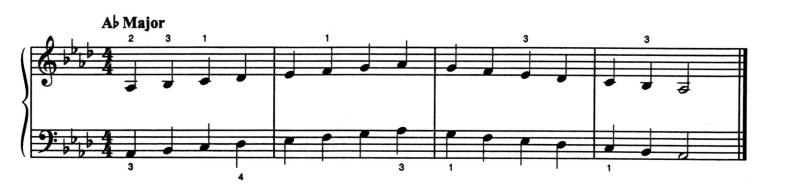

D♭ Major

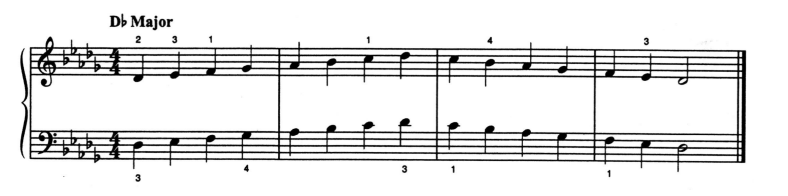

G♭ Major

HARMONIC MINOR SCALES - ONE OCTAVE

In the harmonic minor scale the seventh degree is raised a half step, ascending and descending. See page 33 for melodic minor scales.

A Minor

E Minor

B Minor

F# Minor

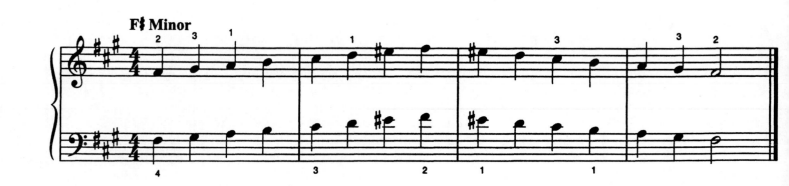

7

C♯ Minor

G♯ Minor

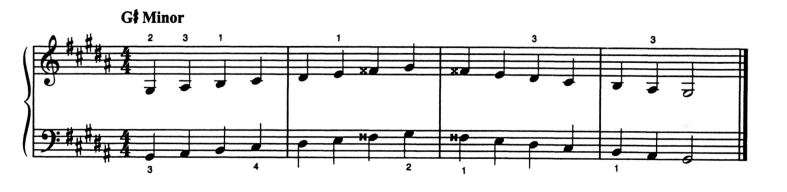

D Minor

G Minor

EL02553A

8

C Minor

F Minor

B♭ Minor

E♭ Minor

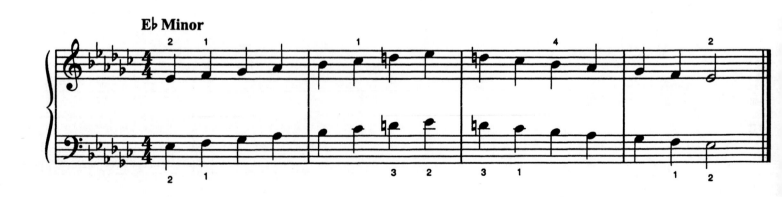

MELODIC MINOR SCALES - ONE OCTAVE

In the melodic minor scale the sixth and seventh degrees are raised a half step ascending and lowered to natural minor descending.

A Minor

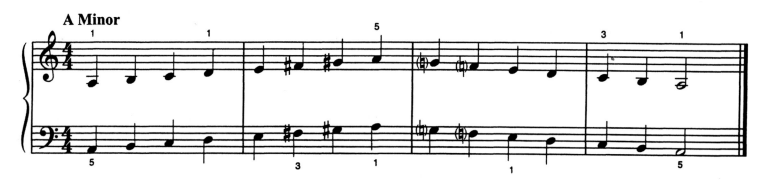

E Minor

B Minor

F♯ Minor

10

C♯ Minor

G♯ Minor

D Minor

G Minor

C Minor

F Minor

Bb Minor

Eb Minor

EL02553A

MAJOR SCALES - TWO OCTAVES

C Major

G Major

D Major

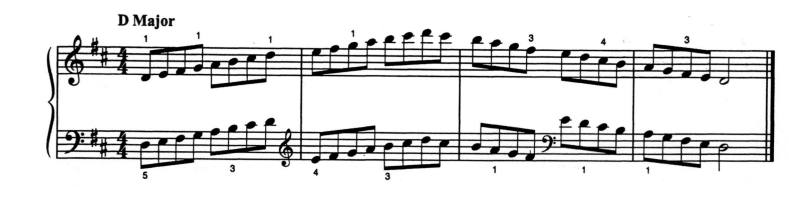

A Major

E Major

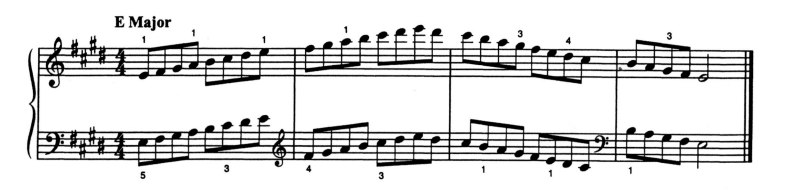

B Major

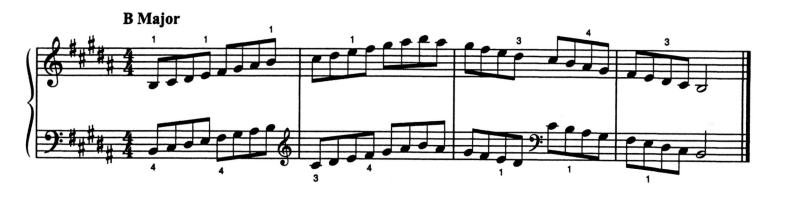

F Major

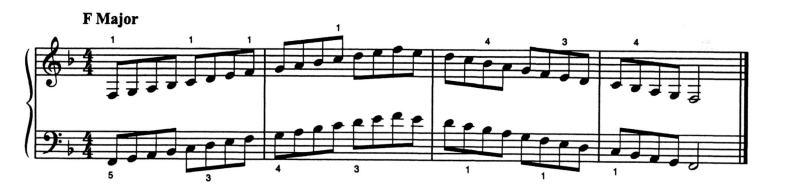

B♭ Major

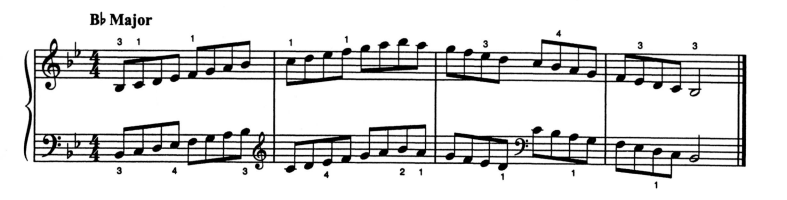

14

HARMONIC MINOR SCALES - TWO OCTAVES

A Minor

E Minor

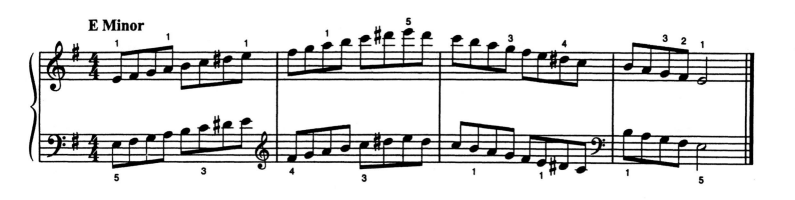

B Minor

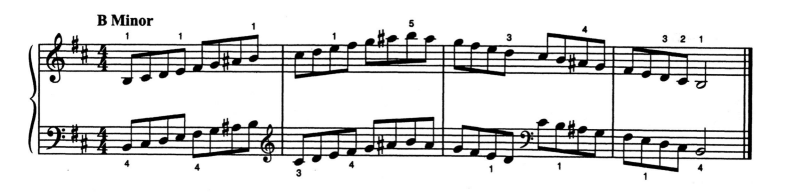

F♯ Minor

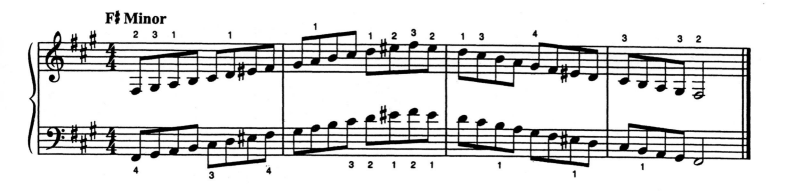

C♯ Minor

G♯ Minor

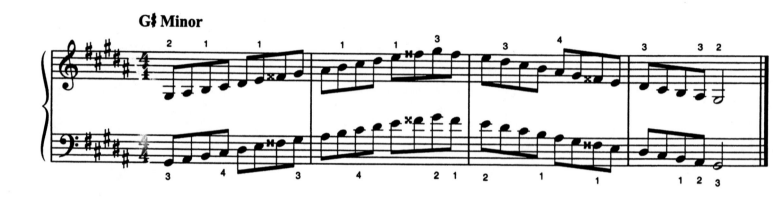

D Minor

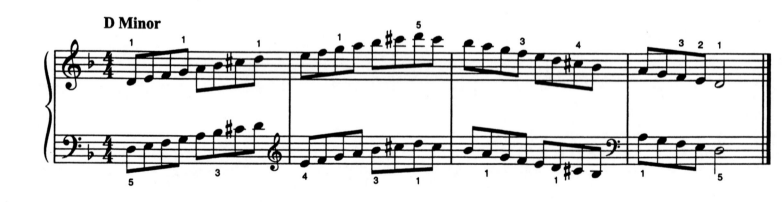

G Minor

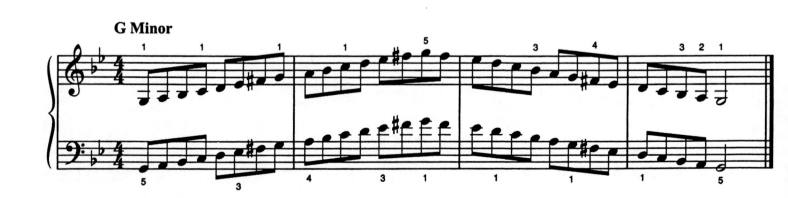

C Minor

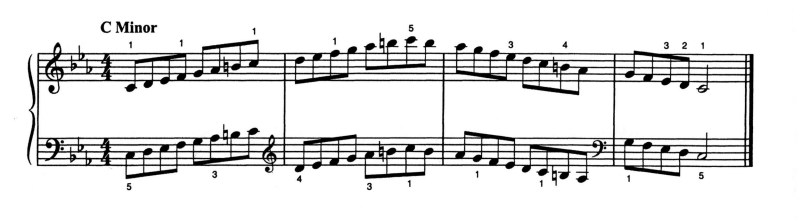

F Minor

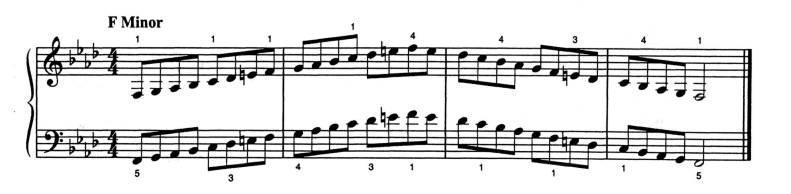

B♭ Minor

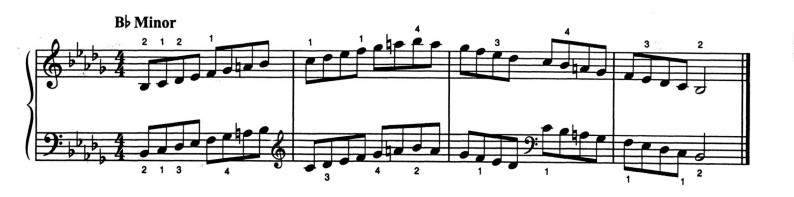

E♭ Minor

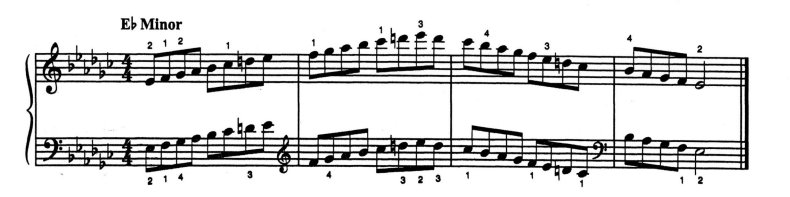

MAJOR SCALES - THREE OCTAVES

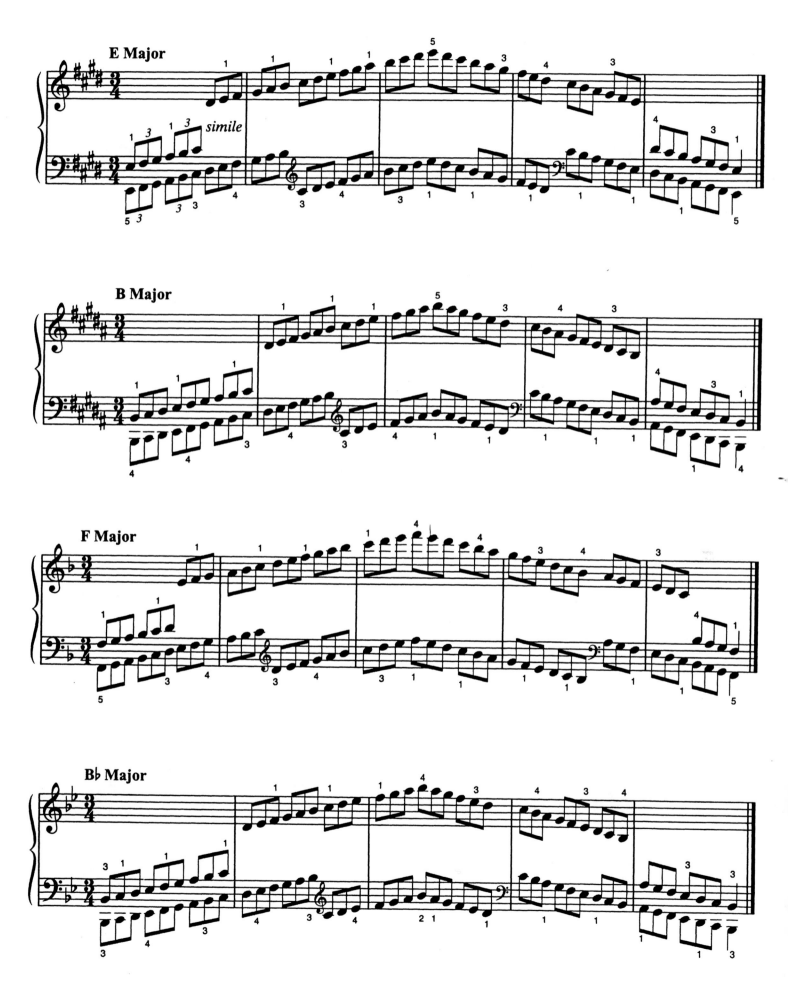

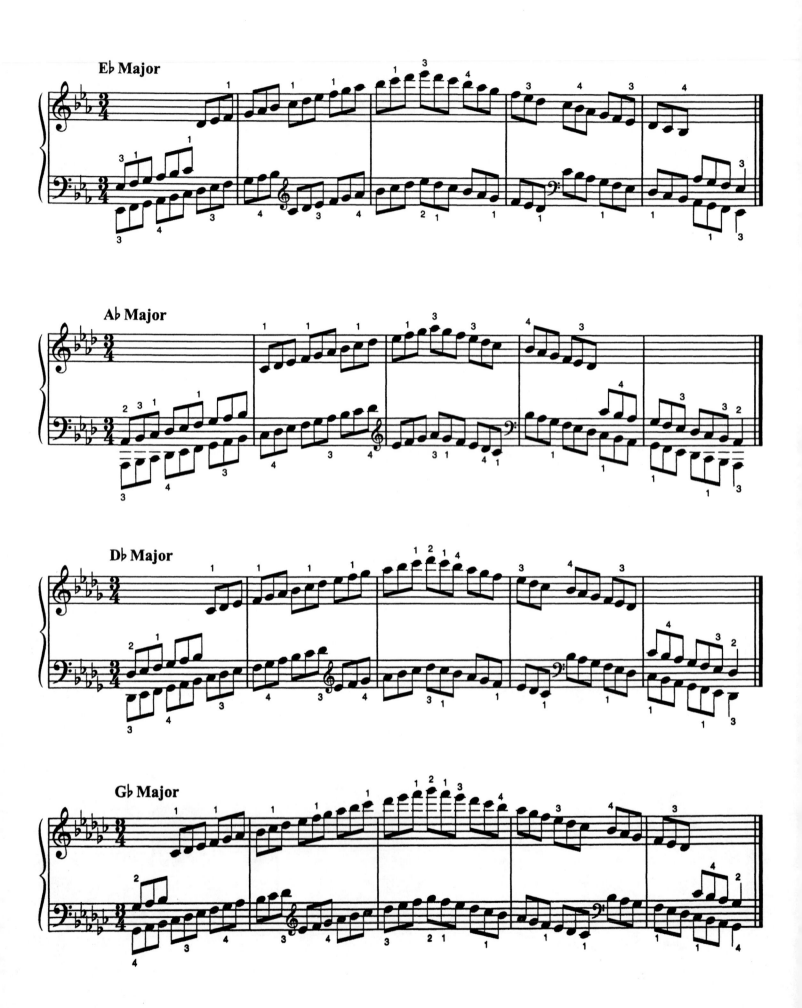

HARMONIC MINOR SCALES - THREE OCTAVES

22

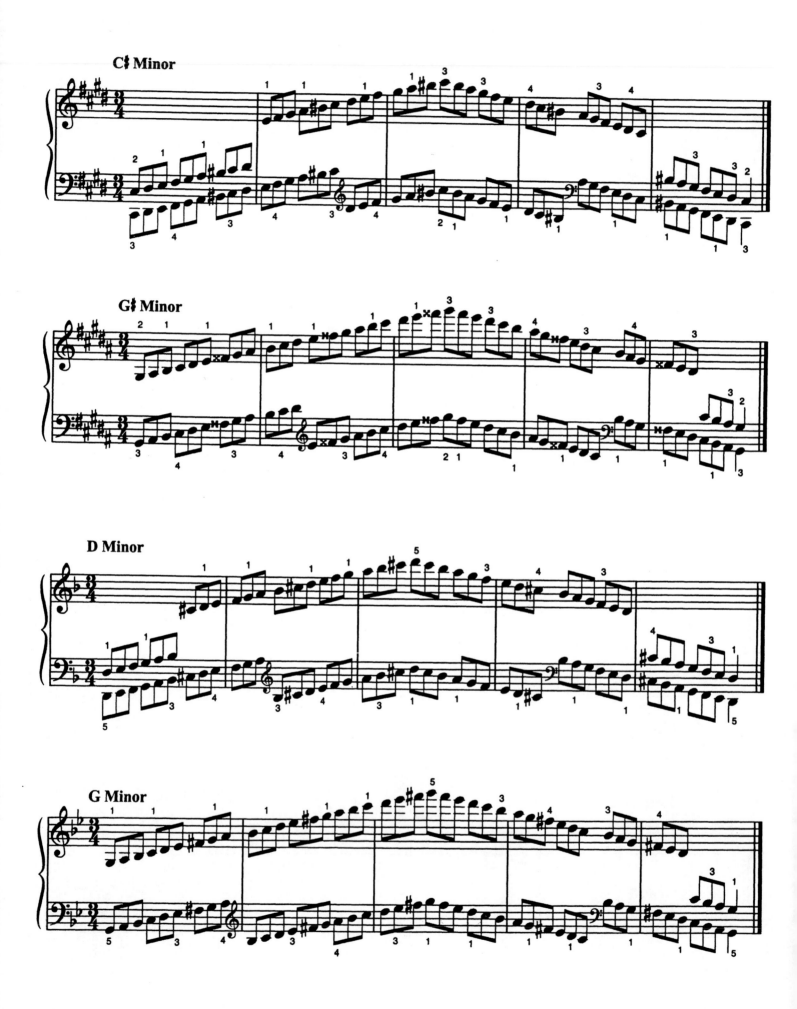

EL02553A

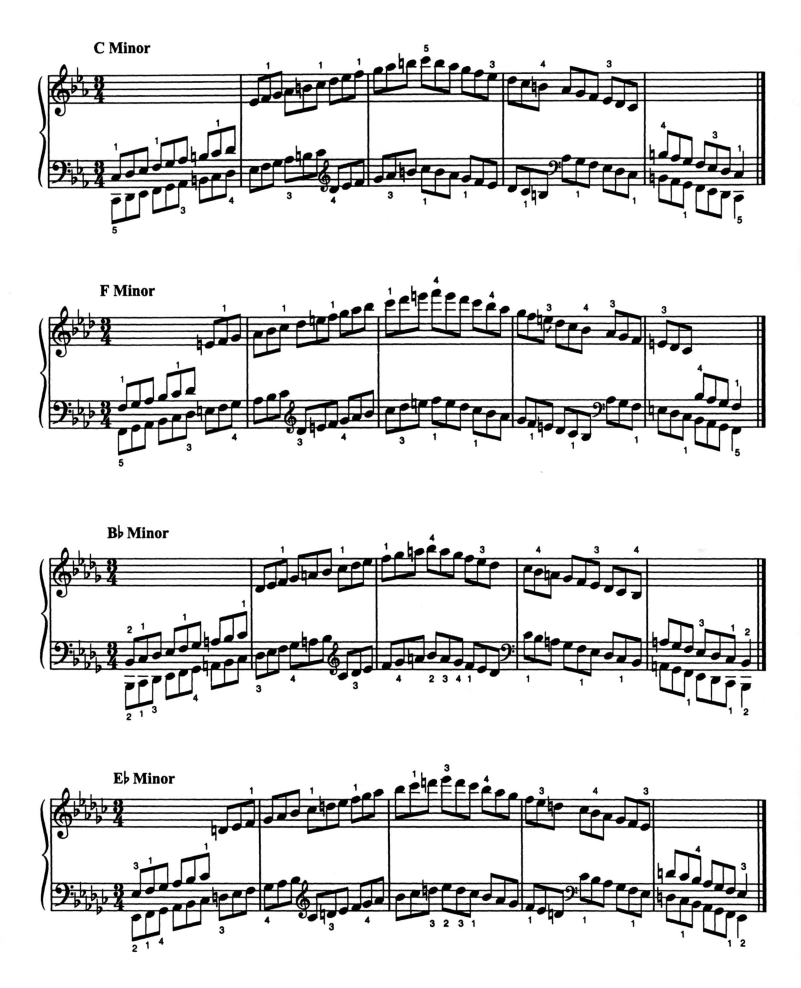

MAJOR SCALES - FOUR OCTAVES

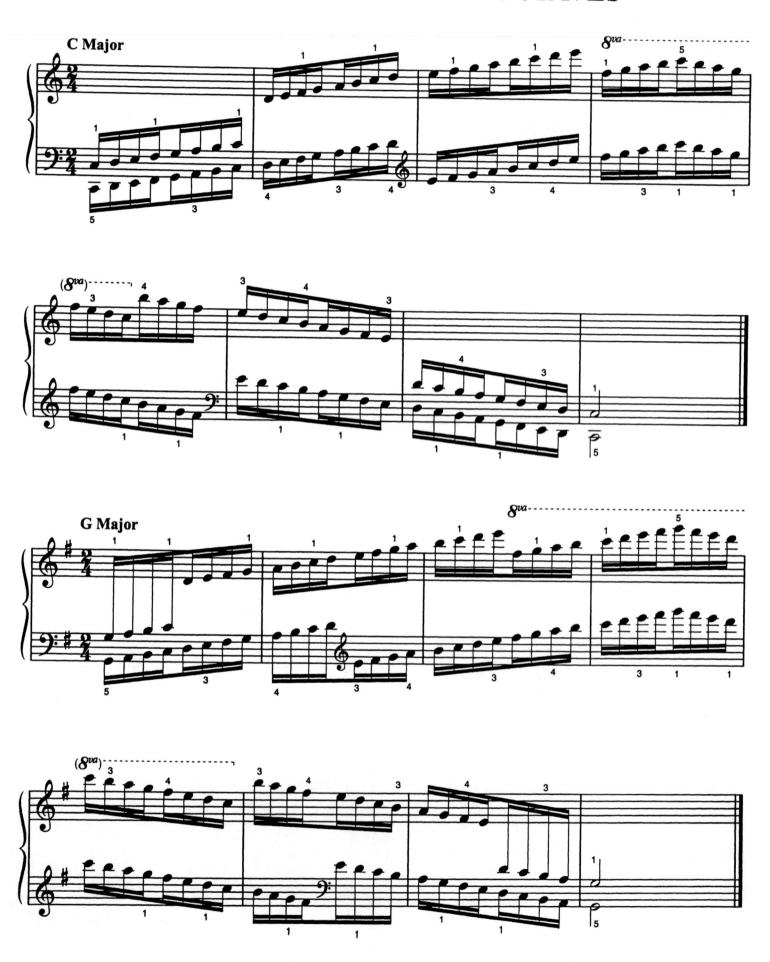

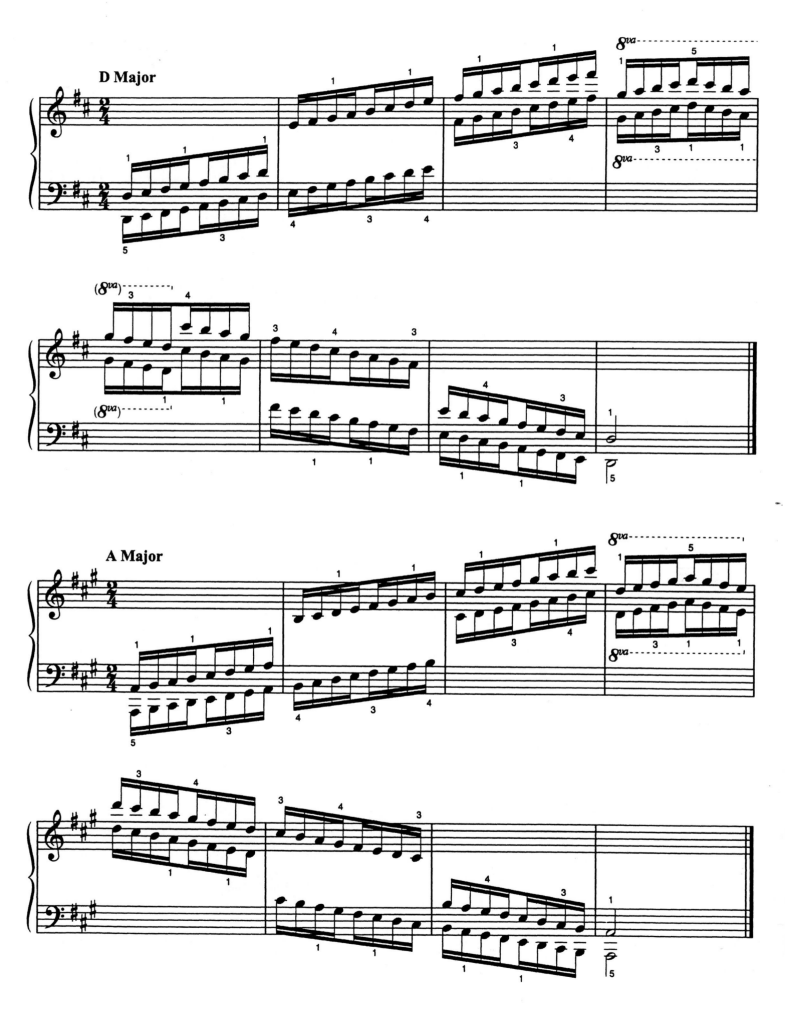

D Major

A Major

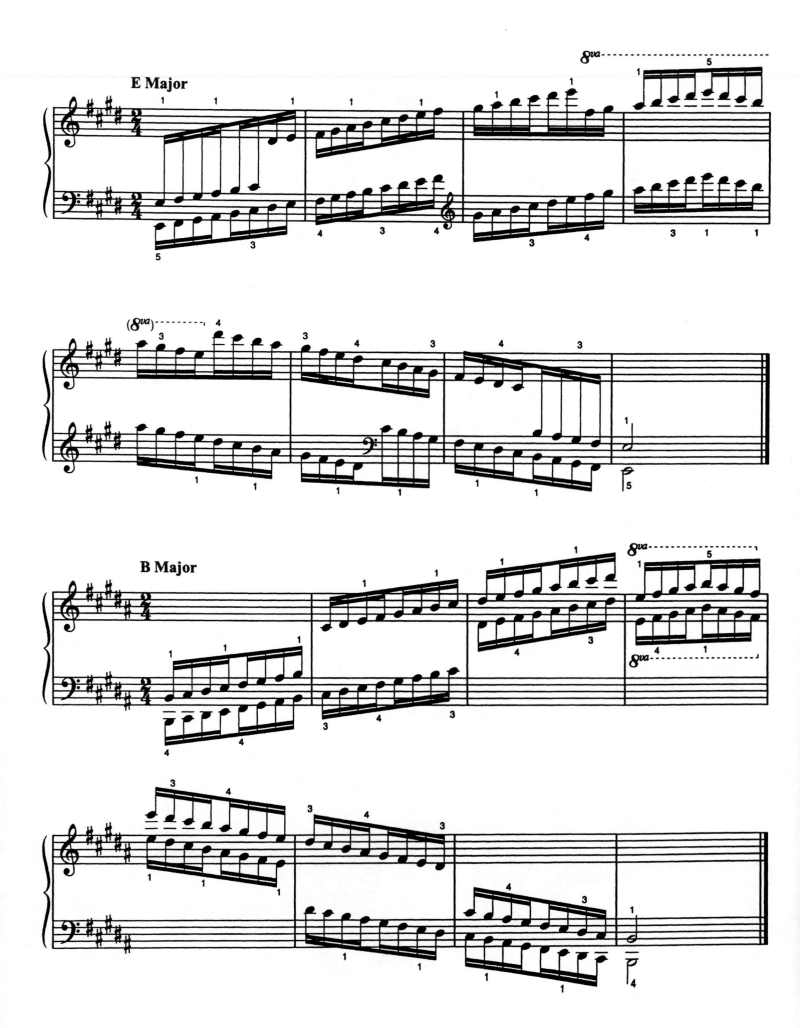

E Major

B Major

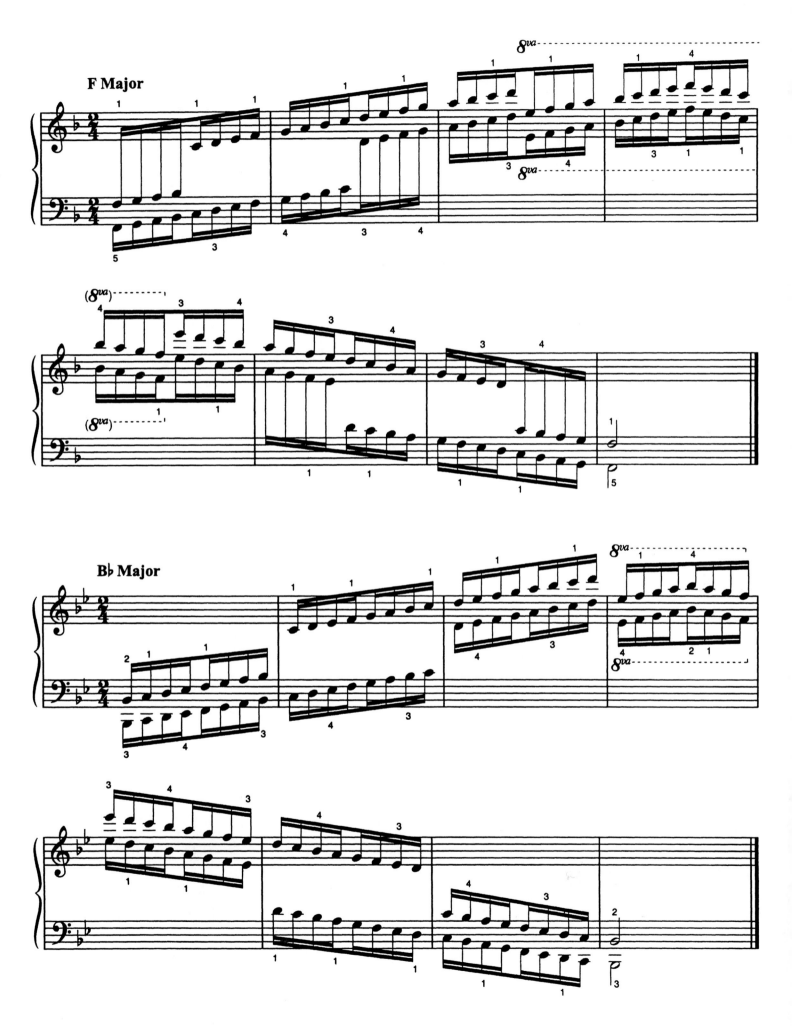

28

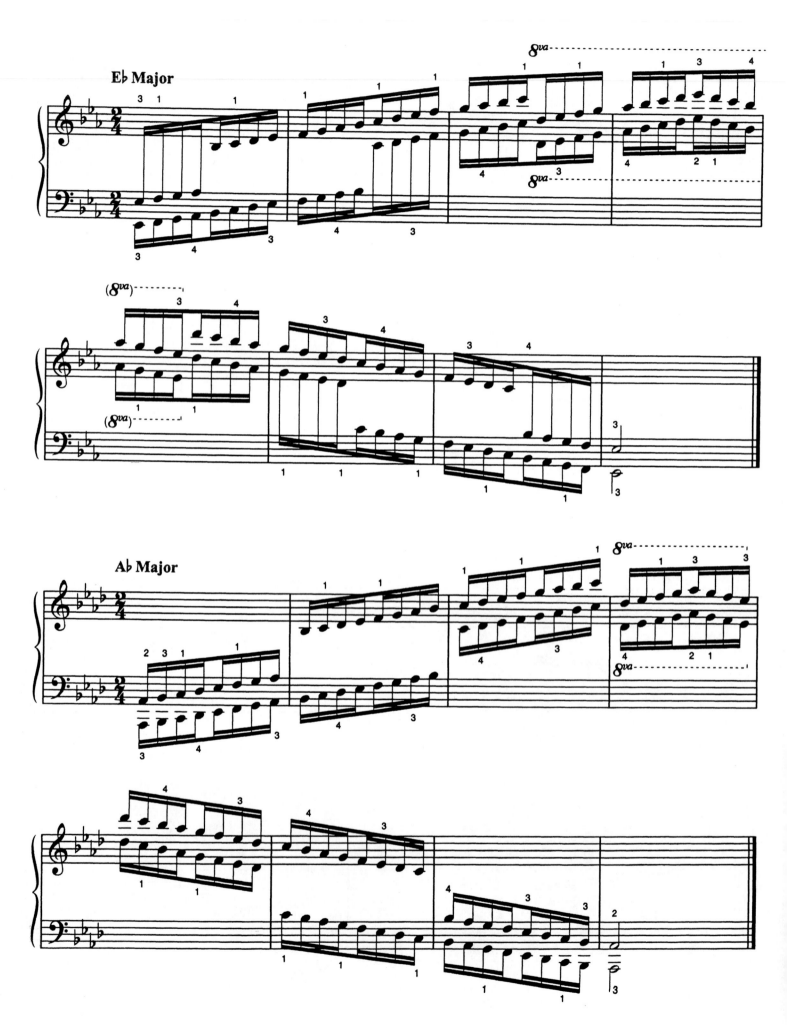

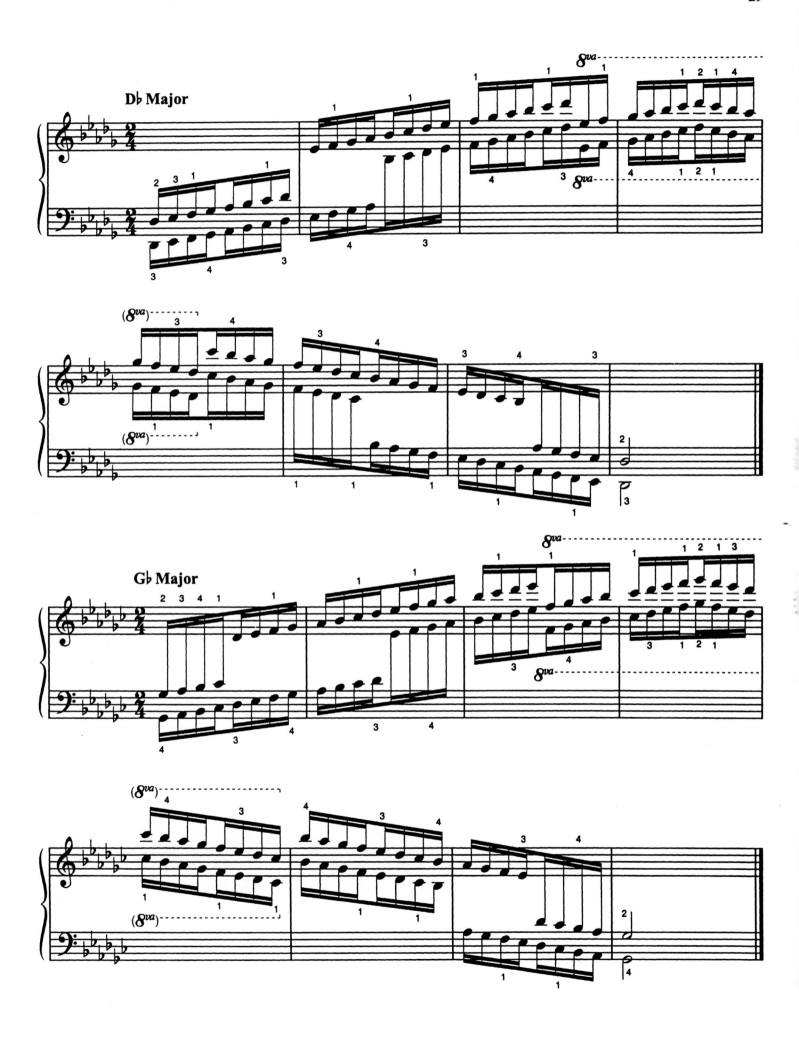

HARMONIC MINOR SCALES - FOUR OCTAVES

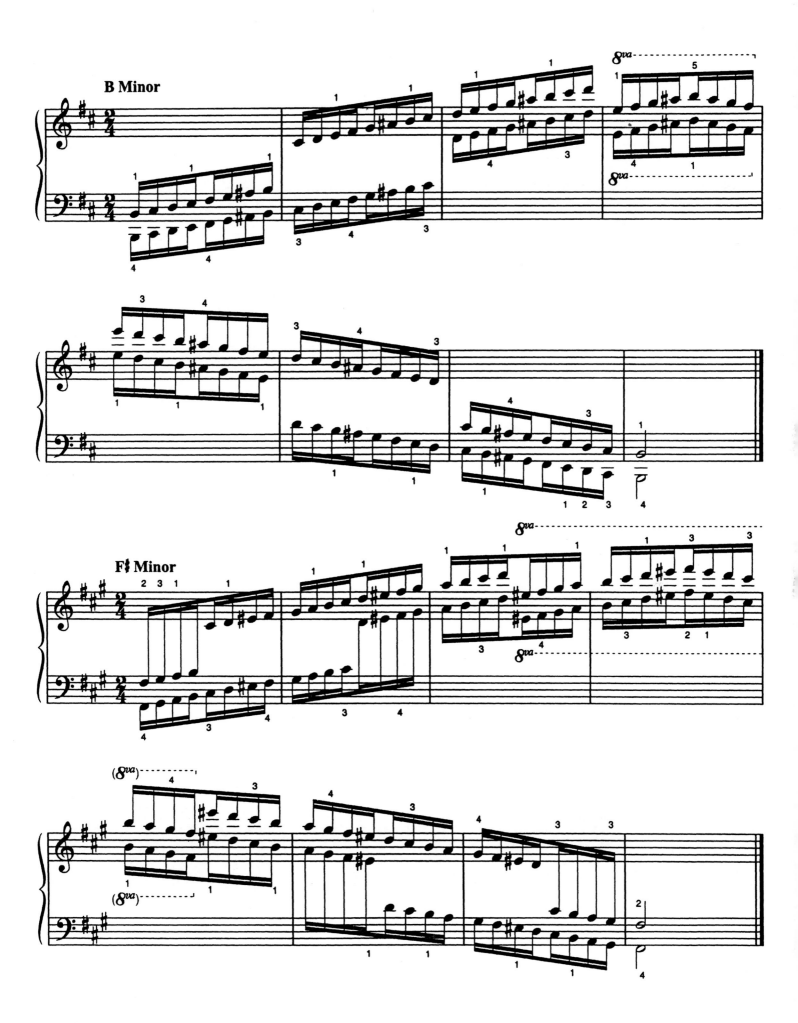

32

C♯ Minor

G♯ Minor

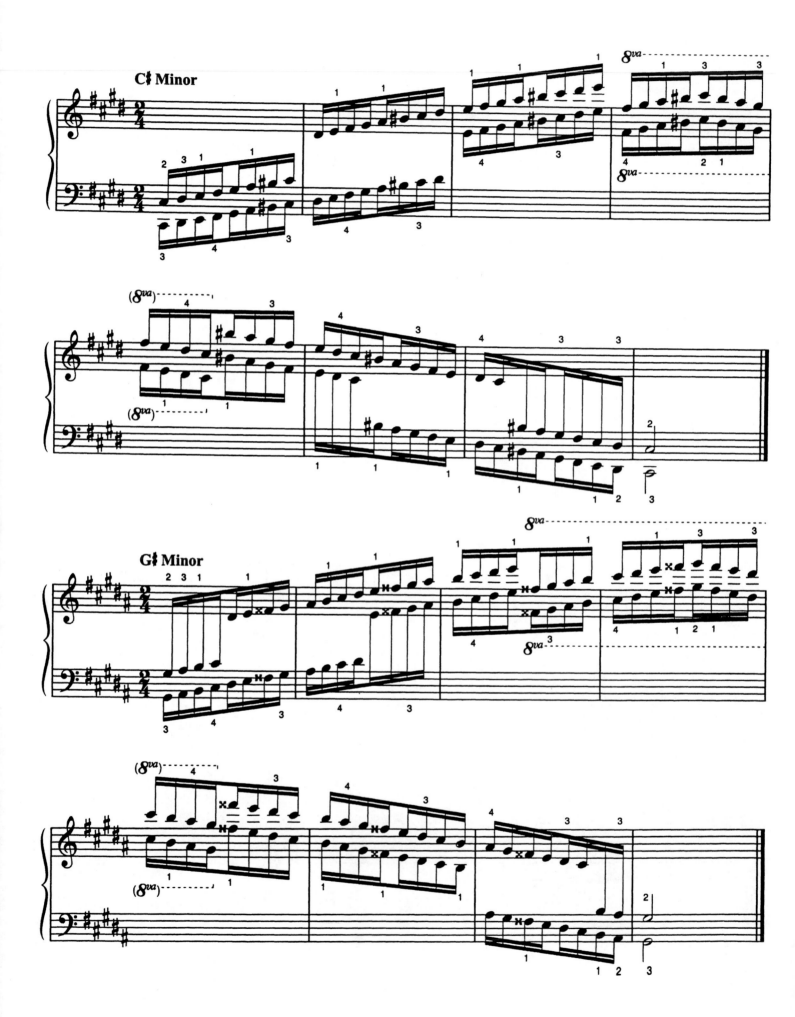

EL02553A

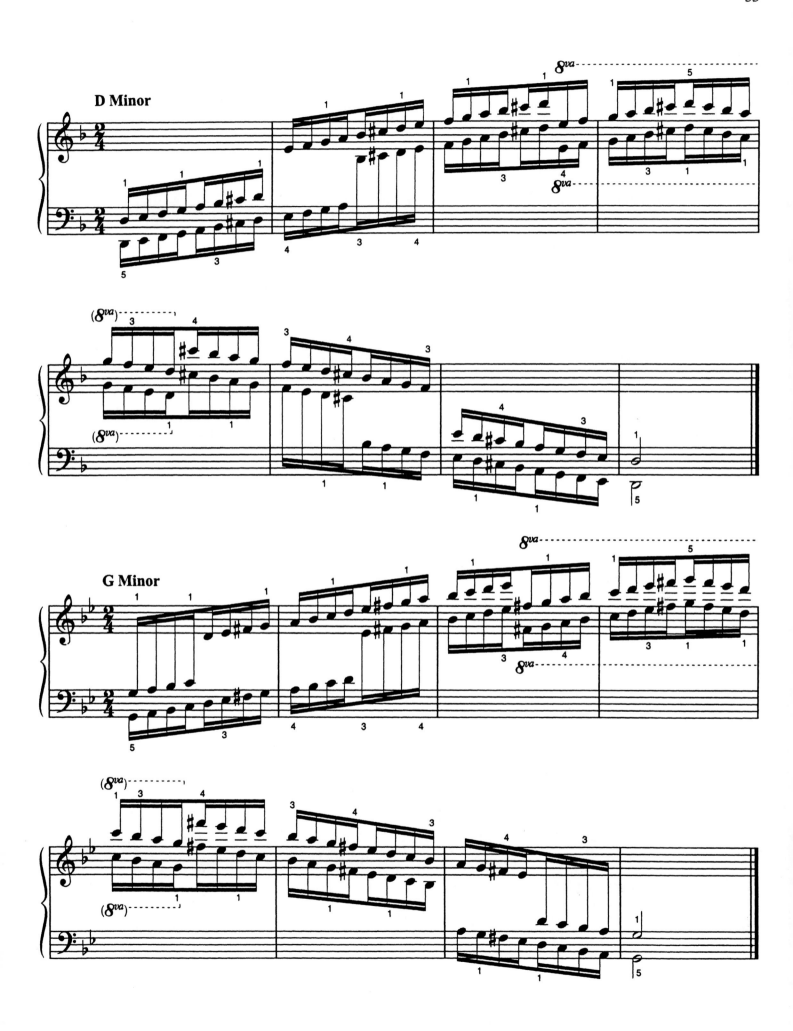

34

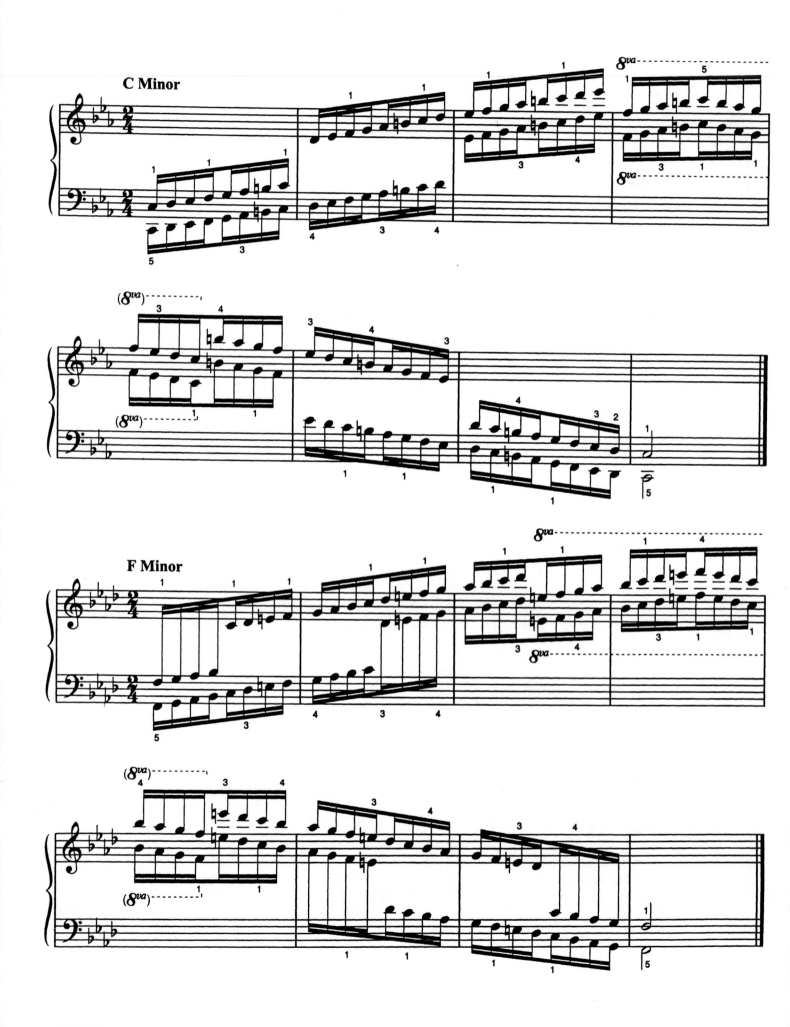

C Minor

F Minor

EL02553A

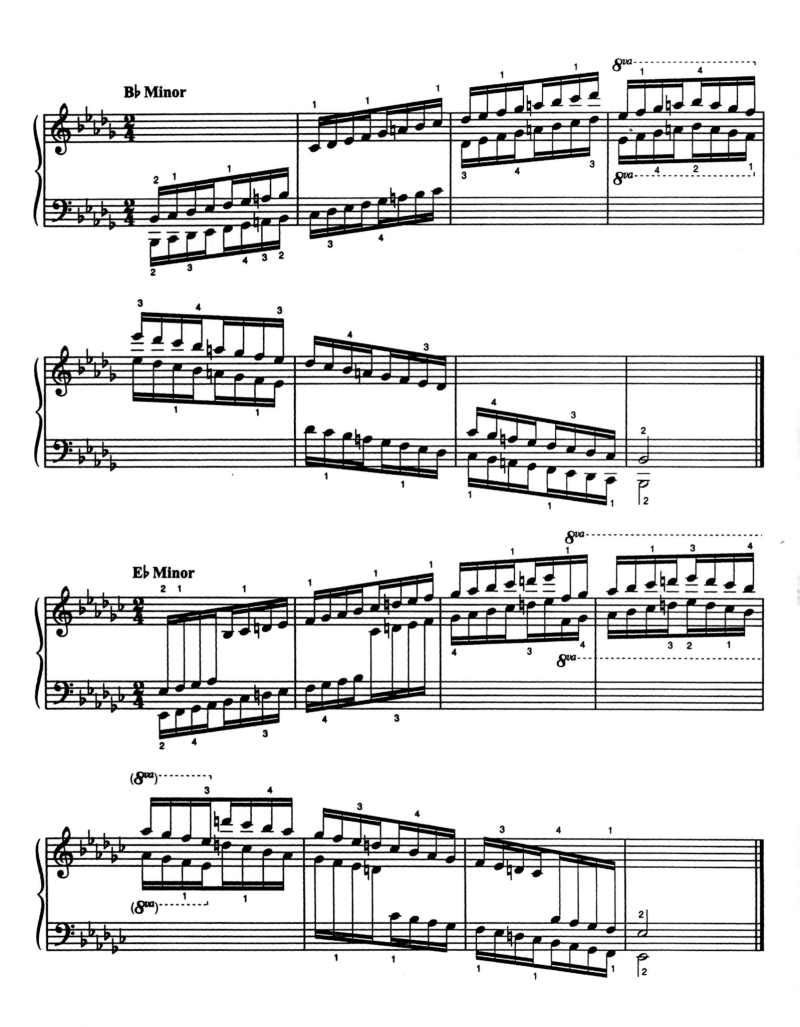

Technic Is Fun

Graded Etude Collections from Standard Repertory

Elementary A (ELM00035) ......Early Elementary
compiled and edited by Gail Lew

Elementary B (EL02495A) ......Preparatory
compiled and edited by David Hirschberg

Book One (EL02496A) ....Late Elementary
compiled and edited by David Hirschberg

Book Two (EL02497A) ....Early Intermediate
compiled and edited by David Hirschberg

Book Three (EL02498A) ....Intermediate
compiled and edited by David Hirschberg

Book Four (EL02499A) ....Late Intermediate
compiled and edited by David Hirschberg

Book Five (EL02500A) ....Early Advanced
compiled and edited by Gail Lew

Technic Is Fun offers piano students a series of graded studies and etudes for the development of technic, style, and musicianship. These studies will reinforce the technical requirements found in method books and in standard piano repertory. The etudes found in this series not only build technic and musicality but also have been carefully selected to provide refreshing recital repertoire and to develop a strong musical and technical foundation.